NOW YOU CAN READ. . . .
WONDERFUL EASTER

STORY RETOLD BY LEONARD MATTHEWS

ILLUSTRATED BY CLIVE UPTTON

Library of Congress Cataloging in Publication Data

Matthews, Leonard.
  Wonderful Easter

  (Now you can read—Bible stories)
  Summary: Retells the Bible story of the resurrection
of Jesus and his appearances to Mary Magdalene and the
disciples.
  1. Jesus Christ—Resurrection—Juvenile literature.
[1. Jesus Christ—Resurrection. 2. Easter. 3. Bible
stories—N.T.] I. Title. II. Series.
BT481.M375 1984   232.9'7   84-9846
ISBN 0-86625-312-2

GROLIER ENTERPRISES CORP.

NOW YOU CAN READ....
WONDERFUL EASTER

"Three days after I die, I shall rise again." That is what Jesus promised to His friends. He died on the cross on a Friday. His body was taken to a cave in a big garden. The people who did not like Jesus wanted to be sure no one would see Him again. They put a huge stone across the entrance to the cave. The next day, Saturday, was the Jews' day of rest. It was called the Sabbath. Everywhere was quiet.

Suddenly, during the night, a noise was heard. There was a long, low rumbling and the earth began to shake. Something very strange was happening.

Some soldiers who were guarding the cave ran, shaking with fear. By dawn on Sunday, all was quiet again. Then, some women carrying lighted lanterns walked toward the cave. They were led by Mary Magdalene, who had been a friend of Jesus.

When Jesus was laid to rest in the cave, His body had been covered with soft white clothes. The women were bringing spices to sprinkle on those clothes. The sun was rising when they reached the cave.

The women had wondered if they
were strong enough to roll aside the
great stone that blocked the door to
the cave.

Perhaps some of the men friends
of Jesus would help them.

Imagine their surprise when they
saw that the stone had already been
moved to one side.

Mary Magdalene stepped inside the cave. There, sitting on the right side was a young man. He was wearing a long, white robe. His face shone.

Mary shook with fear. The young man spoke to her.

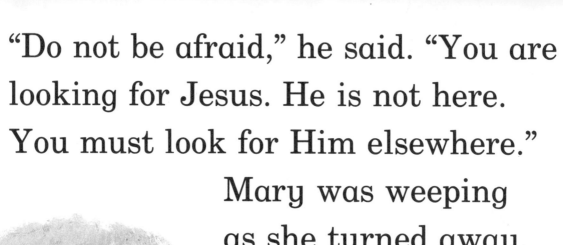

"Do not be afraid," he said. "You are looking for Jesus. He is not here. You must look for Him elsewhere."

Mary was weeping as she turned away. Then she saw a man standing near her.

"Tell me why you are weeping?"
the stranger asked.
Mary thought he must be a
gardener.

"I weep because my Lord and
Master has been taken away," she
replied, "and I do not know where He
has been taken."

The man spoke her name. "Mary."
Now she knew who
He was. "Master!"
she cried. "No, do not
touch me," He
said. "Instead go
and tell our
friends you have
seen me." Mary
hurried away to
spread the news.

That same afternoon two friends of Jesus were walking toward a village called Emmaus.
They were talking about Mary's visit to the cave.

In the dim light of early evening, a stranger joined them.
"Why are you so sad?" He asked.

"Our friend Jesus died on the cross on Friday," said one of the men. "This morning we heard that Mary Magdalene and some other women went to the cave where He was laid. He was not there. Now He is lost to us."

"Surely you have heard that Jesus would rise again from the dead," said the stranger. "He would rise on the third day after He died." He talked to the men until they reached Emmaus. They did not know that the stranger was Jesus.

Night was falling. The two men had agreed to stay the night in Emmaus. Jesus said goodbye to them.

"Why not stay here with us?" the men asked. Jesus nodded and agreed. They ate together in an inn.

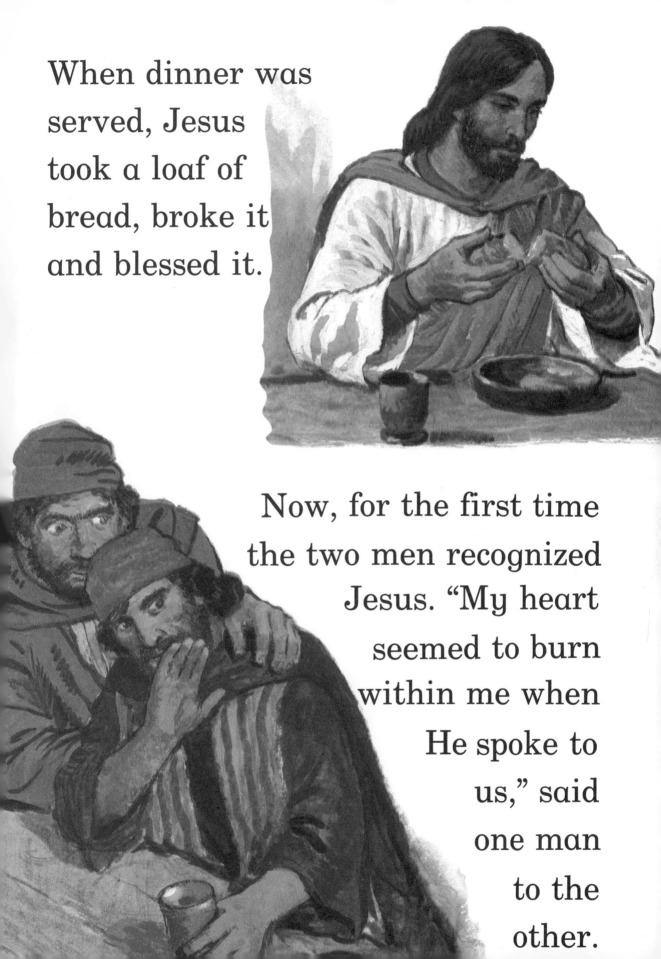

When dinner was served, Jesus took a loaf of bread, broke it and blessed it.

Now, for the first time the two men recognized Jesus. "My heart seemed to burn within me when He spoke to us," said one man to the other.

Even as he said this, the figure
of Jesus disappeared. Quickly, the
two men left the inn and rushed

back to Jerusalem. There, they
found other disciples. "We have
talked with Jesus," they said.

The disciples
were surprised.
Suddenly, Jesus
was among
them. Jesus
held out His
hands. On each
were the scars
of the nails that
had been driven
into His hands
on the cross.
Now they knew
He had kept His
promise: "In
three days
I shall
rise
again."

They were no longer afraid. They
knew that here with them was their
friend and master, Jesus. Then, as so
often before, He sat and ate with
them. Afterward, He led them out
into the country.
There, He said
His last goodbye.
He left them and
went to heaven.

Every year now, we celebrate Easter and Jesus's ascension. We think about that wonderful time when Jesus rose from the dead!

All these appear in the pages of the story. Can you find them?

Jesus

Emmaus

cave

Mary
Magdalene

friends of
Jesus

Now tell the story in your own words.